candlelight, moonlight, all shining bright.

I see you
and you see me.
LIGHT is the reason
we can see.

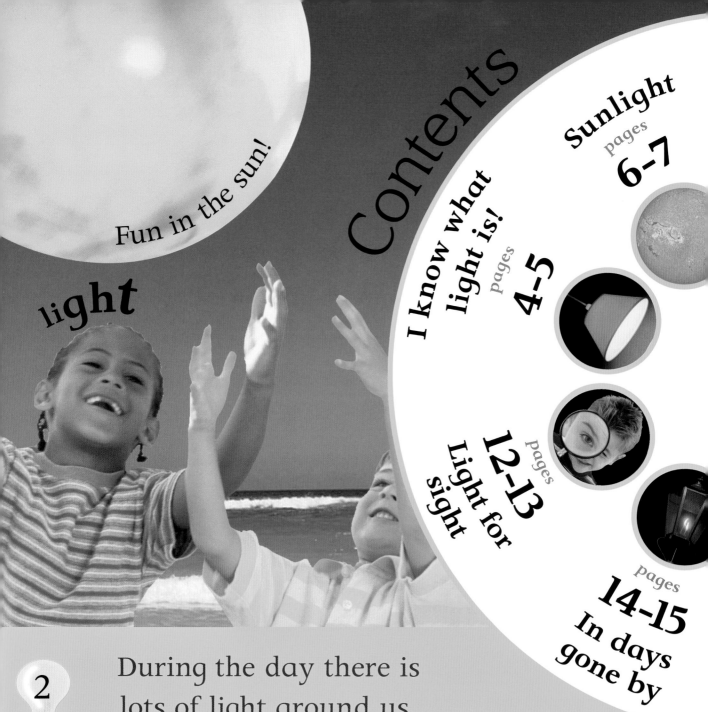

light

Fun in the sun!

Contents

During the day there is lots of light around us.

2

If there were no light then life would be like sitting in a very dark room at night. We need light to see.

dark

At night the light goes and it gets dark.

I know what

I know that light is
the opposite of dark.

The Sun

The Sun in the sky gives us light, even when it is cloudy. But it only gives us light during the day. At night the Sun disappears and it gets dark.

All plants and animals need
light to live, including you and me.

Shadow play

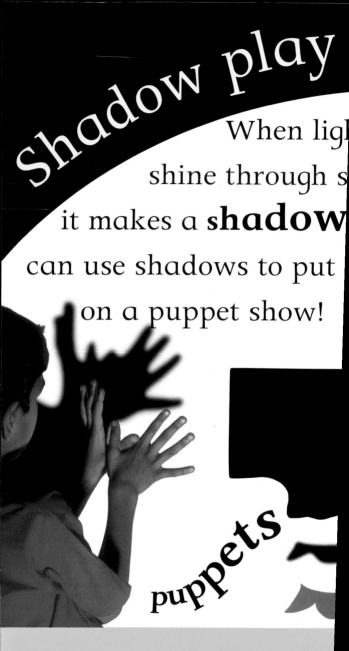

When lig[ht]
shine through s[omething]
it makes a **shadow**[. You]
can use shadows to put
on a puppet show!

puppets

A shadow is the dark a[rea]
something that blocks o[ut]

How to make a shadow puppet

You will need:
Poster board
Pencil
Scissors
Tape
Thin stick
A wall in a
  dark room
Flashlight

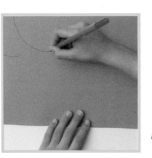

1. Draw the shape of an animal on poster board.

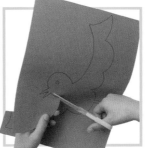

2. Cut out the shape.

3. Tape the puppet to one end of the stick.

Puppet show

Turn out the lights and turn on your flashlight. Shine the flashlight onto a wall. Wave your puppet between the flashlight and the wall for a shadow-puppet show.

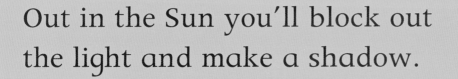

Out in the Sun you'll block out the light and make a shadow.

star

In a spin

Although we can't feel it, our Earth spins around all the time. In fact, it spins in a whole circle in 24 hours, or one day.

What is night?

As the Earth spins, part of it faces the Sun, where light shines on it and gives us daylight. The part that is facing away from the Sun, where there is no light, is in darkness—night. So when it is day in New York City it is night in Hong Kong.

star

tars shine because they are very, very hot, which makes them light up.

Good light

Green plants, like grass, use the sunlight that **shines** on their leaves to make food.

butterfly

cow

We use sun on our skin to make vitamin D. This keeps us healthy.

Light for life

Nothing can live
without sunlight.
You, me, **plants**,
and animals all need it.

butterfly

grass

Plants need
light to
live.

Animals
eat plants
to live.

People eat
plants and
animals
to live.

Plants need sunlight
and water to grow.

Safe in the Sun

Too much sun can burn your skin. So protect yourself when you go out in the sunlight.

sun

remember!

Slip
...on
a shirt

Slap
...on
a hat

...on some
sunscreen

Cover up or play in the shade.

flying owl

firefly

Fireflies

Fireflies are tiny insects that can make their own light in their bodies. If you see hundreds of little dots of light flying around after dark, they could be fireflies. Fireflies use the light to send messages to each other.

Owls can fly and hunt in complete darkness without bumping into anything!

Animals at night

Some animals wake up and are active at night. They have different **eyes** from us—they can see in the dark.

Owls' eyes

Owls have huge eyes so they can see at night much better than we can.

Owls can turn their heads around fully to see behind them.

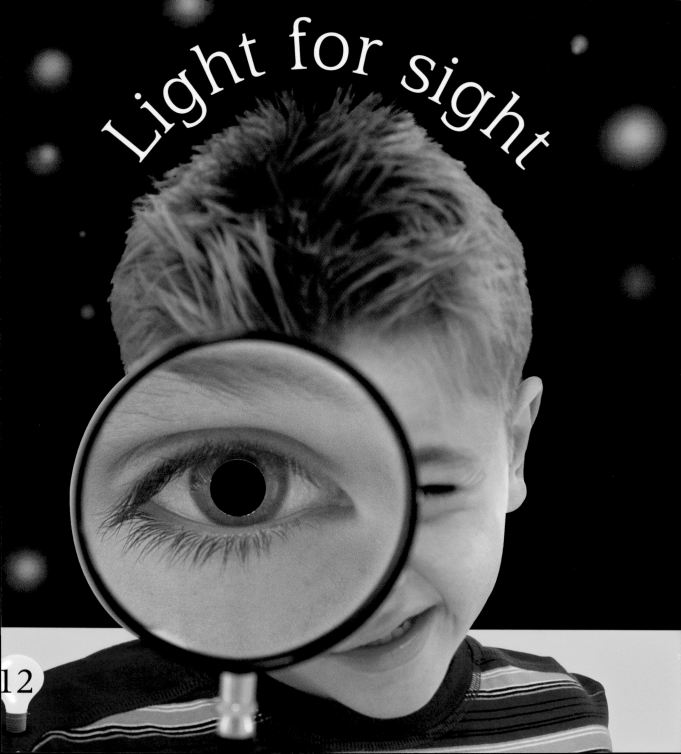

Light for sight

12

We see best when there is lots of light around. That's because our eyes need **light** to see. Try this test to see how our eyes take in light.

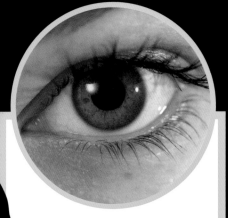

Eye test

1. Look in a mirror. See the black circle in the center of your eye. This is called a pupil.

2. Now sit with your hands over your eyes for one minute.

3. Open your eyes and quickly look at your pupil again. Is it bigger than before? Pupils get bigger in the dark to let in more light.

Light goes into our eyes through black holes called pupils, and we can see.

In days gone by

Imagine if there were no lights to switch on at night and no **streetlights** along the roads. That's what life was like for thousands of years. So how did the people who lived in the past see after dark?

From the beginning of time people have needed light to see. Here are some ways they lit up the night.

Fire

More than 10,000 years ago people used fire to keep themselves warm and to see in the dark. They set fire to wood, which they used as torches.

Gaslight

In 1813 the first streetlight
was lit in London, England.
It used gas and had to be lit
by hand every single night!

Candles

Candles were first used to light
up houses in the 1300s. People had to
carry candles to find their way to bed.

Some candles
are made from
wax made by bees.

candle

Oil lamps

Oil lamps were used 2,000 years ago and right
up to about 120 years ago. Each one had a wick,
like a candle, that was dipped in oil and lit.

Electric light

These days, when it gets **dark** and the Sun is not shining, what do we do? We switch on a light! A light bulb uses something called electricity to **shine** brightly for us to see.

light bulb

Turn on a light bulb

In the late 1800s, only about 120 years ago, a man called Thomas Edison developed the light bulb, which changed the world. He flicked the first light switch in New York City.

When electricity was invented homes and streets were **lit** up at night. Before that nights were very dark.

Flick the switch!

...the world

Dark areas have
few people and lights.

A world of lights

There are so many lights on at night that you can see them from space. Can you tell where the cities are?

Light up...

Cities have the most lights on at night so are the most brightly lit places.

Festivals of light

Light is very important in many religions. It is used for decoration and celebration during festivals.

Diwali

Diwali is the Hindu festival of light. Candles are lit to celebrate the Hindu new year.

Christmas

Christians around the world use lights to decorate Christmas trees.

Hanukkah

During the Jewish festival of Hanukkah, candles are lit at dusk for eight days.

In China thousands of lanterns are lit at the end of the Chinese new year celebrations.

Lights for safety
Traffic lights make sure people don't bump into each other on roads.

Everyday light

Light for energy
We even use light from the Sun to make electricity that lights our houses.

Look around you during the day and when it gets dark. You will notice lights everywhere.

Lights to guide
Lighthouses shine lights at night to warn ships to keep away from rocks.

Lights to talk
Signal indicators on our cars tell people when we are about to turn a corner.

City lights

At night a city looks completely different because of all the lights.
Not only do we use them to find our way, but also to decorate
buildings and to light up stores and restaurants.

TAXI
OFF   DUTY

headlights

Headlights on cars
light up the road ahead.

brakelight

Lights are used for decoration on buildings and on huge advertisements.

DK

LONDON, NEW YORK, MUNICH, MELBOURNE, and DELHI

Written by
Penelope Arlon
Edited by
Penny Smith
Designed by
Cathy Chesson

DTP designer: Almudena Díaz
Production: Claire Pearson
Publishing manager: Sue Leonard
Art director: Rachael Foster

First American Edition, 2006
Published in the United States by
DK Publishing, Inc., 375 Hudson Street,
New York, New York 10014

06 07 08 09 10 10 9 8 7 6 5 4 3 2 1
Copyright © 2006 Dorling Kindersley Ltd.

A Cataloging-in-Publication record for this book is available from the Library of Congress.

ISBN-10: 0-7566-2225-5
ISBN-13: 978-0-7566-2225-1

Color reproduction by Media Development and Printing, United Kingdom
Printed and bound in China by
Hung Hing Off-set Printing Co., Ltd

Discover more at
www.dk.com

Picture Credits

The publisher would like to thank the following for their kind permission to reproduce their photographs:
(Key: a-above; b-below/bottom; c-center; f-far; l-left; r-right; t-top; bg-background.)
Alamy Images: ImageState 2cra, 5cl; Adrian Muttitt 8 (Window); Daniel Templeton 2fcrb, 15r (Gas Lamp); Transtock Inc. 18-19 (Red Car). **Ancient Art & Architecture Collection:** Prisma 14 (Cave). **The Art Archive:** Dagli Orti 15r (Table). **Bridgeman Art Library:** Barbara Singer 15 (Girl A/W). **Corbis:** 2 (Sky), 3br, 3fclb, 4 (Background), 10 (Butterfly), 10-11 (Sea), 17 (Switch), 20-21t; M. Angelo 8 (Wall); Craig Aurness 4cr; Gareth Brown 18-19 (Lanterns); Amit Dave/Reuters 18clb; Pat Doyle 9 (Dog); Owen Franken 8 (Shutters); Karl-Heinz Haenel/zefa 9 (Sunflowers), 20-21b; Kevin King; Ecoscene 3cla, 10 (Cow); Howard Kingsnorth/ zefa endpaper t; Matthias Kulka/zefa 3tr, 5; LWA- JDC 3clb, 18cb; P. Manner/zefa 10 (Meadow); Newmann/zefa 13cla, 13cra; Reza; Webistan 9l (Puppet); Jim Richardson endpaper b; Guenter Rossenbach/zefa 10 (Grass); Tom Stewart 2l; Brad Swonetz/zefa 3r (Background); Brigitte Sporrer/zefa 9 (Girl); Joson/ zefa 9 (Path). **FLPA - images of nature:** Shin Yoshino/Minden Pictures 13 (Owl). **Getty Images:** Iconica 3fcla, 8 (Boy), 19 (Taxi); The Image Bank 10 (Girl), 13cb, 18crb; Johner Images 1crb; Nordic Photos 19 (Traffic Light); Photographer's Choice 19 (Skyline); Photonica 12 (Firefly), 16r; Stockbyte Platinum 4cl; Stone 11 (Girls), 19 (Billboards); Taxi 19 (L/House). **Science Photo Library:** Tony Craddock 19 (solar panel); Gusto 2crb, 12b; NASA GSFC 17 (Earth); NOAO 2fcra, 6l (Sun); Tom Van Sant/Geosphere Project, Santa Monica 7clb, 7tr.

Jacket images: *Front:* **Corbis:** bl. **Getty Images:** Johner Images c. **Science Photo Library:** Tony Craddock cla. *Back:* **Corbis:** Randy Faris cla; Craig Tuttle clb. *Spine:* **Corbis:** cb; Randy Faris bc. **Science Photo Library:** Tony Craddock ca.

All other images © Dorling Kindersley
For further information see: www.dkimages.com